DATE DUE

DEMCO, INC. 38-2931

TRUE**NORTH**

NEW ALASKAN ARCHITECTURE

BRAUN

Imprint

The Deutsche Nationalbibliothek lists this publication in the Deutsche Na-
tionalbibliografie; detailed bibliographical data are available on the internet
at http://dnb.d-nb.de.

ISBN 978-3-03768-020-9

© 2010 by Braun Publishing AG

1st edition 2010

Editorial staff: Annika Schulz, Sophie Steybe
Graphic concept and layout: Michaela Prinz

TRUE**NORTH**
NEW ALASKAN ARCHITECTURE

JULIE DECKER

BRAUN

CONTENTS

FOREWORD

By Julie Decker

True North is a look at contemporary Alaskan architecture designed for rural and urban areas in a state known for its northern and often extreme environment. While responding to function, the projects featured within also illustrate innovative and sensitive materials palettes, sophisticated forms, and intelligent responses to their sites, natural light and the North. In 2008, Juhani Pallasmaa, noted architect and professor and a resident of the northern city of Helsinki, Finland, twice visited Alaska, touring the land and the architecture. It was these visits that informed his essay for this publication and helped to describe the birth of new design traditions specific to this northern place. Alaska is the largest state in the United States by area, situated in the northwest extremity of the North American continent, bordered by Canada to the east, the Arctic Ocean to the north and the Pacific Ocean to the west and south. Russia lies west across the Bering Strait; Alaska's territorial waters touch Russia's territorial waters in the Bering Strait, as the Russian and Alaskan islands are only 3 miles (4.8 kilometers) apart. As it extends into the eastern hemisphere, it is technically both the westernmost and easternmost state in the United States, as well as also being the northernmost.

The projects in the publication represent a sampling of a new architecture across the vast state. While many of the projects are in Anchorage (approximately half of Alaska's 684,000 residents reside there), others can be found in the most rural and remote of places. As of 2009, Alaska remains the least densely populated state of the U.S. But for those residents, learning how to better build and live in the North has become a key design challenge, one many resident architects are keen on meeting. Alaska is at the beginning of a new sophistication and new thought about design for the elements, elements that can only be found in the True North.

INTRODUCTION

By Julie Decker

Some definitions relate the North simply to the characteristic presence of snow and ice; others suggest that 60° Fahrenheit (15.6° Centigrade) latitude or above constitutes "northern", the line at which we find cities such as Anchorage and Helsinki. Adventurers of every field and interest have been drawn to the northern lands of raw, inescapable beauty and extraordinary qualities of life. Missionaries came on missions, explorers came on discovery voyages, artists came on junkets – all were interested in conquering, capturing and conveying the northern mystique. Today it is oil, politics and climate change that draw the interest up the latitudinal scale.

It is increasingly clear that the North is changing. Scientific evidence shows rapid ice melt in the Arctic, and multiple political, economic, strategic and energy issues come into play with along with the changes. Alaska is the only part of the United States that boasts Arctic territory. But the subarctic zones are vast as well. The region is so large (1/5 the size of the continental United States), and diverse ecologically, physiologically, and culturally that any synthesis is gross generalization.

The Arctic and Subarctic are defined as cold climates primarily by mean temperatures and duration of the freezing period that would eliminate precipitation except in a frozen state. The Arctic is that region in which the mean temperature for the warmest month is -50° Fahrenheit (-45.5° Centigrade) and the average annual temperature is no higher than 32° Fahrenheit (0° Centigrade). The Subarctic is the region in which the mean temperature for the coldest month is -32° Fahrenheit

From above to below:
The dew line, c. 1956. Aurora Borealis, or "northern lights," as seen from White Mountain National Recreation Area. Kodiak Island.

(-35.5° Centigrade) and the mean temperature of the warmest month is above 50° Fahrenheit (10° Centigrade). Northern regions are defined by temperature, permafrost, tree lines, and the Arctic Circle. The Arctic Circle is located at 66° 33' N latitude and defines those regions that have 24 hours of sunlight or darkness sometime during the year.

The northeast corner of Alaska is home to the Arctic National Wildlife Refuge (ANWR), which covers 19,049,236 acres (77,090 square kilometers). Alaska includes roughly 23 million acres (93,100 square kilometers) of land. The Arctic is Alaska's most remote wilderness. The National Petroleum Reserve-Alaska is 120 miles (190 kilometers) from any village. Similarly, the Aleutian Islands are so remote that Amchitka Island was chosen in 1971 by the U.S. military as a test site for the detonation of an underground atomic bomb.

Alaska has nearly 34,000 miles (54,720 kilometers) of tidal shoreline and is also home to many active volcanoes (the most volcanoes of any of the fifty U.S. states). Alaska has a longer coastline than all the other U.S. states combined. It is technically part of the continental U.S., but is often not included in colloquial use; residents refer to the contiguous states as "the Lower 48" or "Outside". The state's capital city, Juneau, is situated on the mainland of the North American continent, but is not connected by road to the rest of the North American highway system nor by road to Anchorage, the state's largest city.

One of the world's largest tides occurs in Turnagain Arm, just south of Anchorage – tidal differences can be more than 35 feet (10.7 meters) and Alaska has more than three million lakes. Wetlands and marshlands and wetland permafrost cover 188,320 square miles (487,747 square kilometers). Frozen water, in the form of glacier ice, covers some 16,000 square miles (41,440 square kilometers) of land and 1,200 square miles (3,110 square kilometers) of tidal zone. With over 100,000 of them, Alaska has half of the world's glaciers.

From above to below:
View of downtown Anchorage from the west. Base of Mount McKinley. Aerial view of the Noatak River. Cape Deceit, Seward Peninsula, with the town of Deering in background.

Ten thousand years ago the Alaska mainland was physically and ecologically part of Asia, until it was severed by the rising Bering Sea to the south and the Chukchi Sea to the north. This makes Alaska important to American prehistory – from the early settlement of the continent and as the land through which later waves of immigration passed.

At the time of European contact by the Russian explorers, the area was populated by Alaska Native groups. The name "Alaska" derives from the Aleut word "alaxsxaq" (an archaic spelling being "alyeska"), meaning "mainland" (literally, "the object toward which the action of the sea is directed"). Alaska's Native people are divided into 11 distinct cultures, speaking 11 different languages and 22 different dialects.

The geography of Alaska is dominated by mountains and rivers. Dominating the north of Alaska is the Brooks Range, which runs generally east-west, into the Yukon Territory. Across the center of Alaska runs the Alaska Range, which is dominated by the Denali and Foraker massifs. Lying between the Brooks and Alaska Ranges are the Tanana-Yukon Uplands in the east, and in the far west is the Seward Peninsula. Lowland areas of considerable extent occur on the north slope of Alaska and in the Yukon and Kuskokwim basins of the interior. Southeast Alaska contains the Wrangell Mountains. The Chugach Range runs from that range westward to Prince William Sound and the Kenai Peninsula. In Southwest Alaska, the Aleutian Range is the backdrop to the Alaska Peninsula and continues as the Aleutian Islands, extending about 1,300 miles (2,092 kilometers) into the Bering Sea.

The largest river system is the Yukon and its tributaries, the Porcupine, the Tanana, and the Koyukon. The Yukon crosses Alaska and empties into the Bering Sea. Other rivers and tributaries cross the North Slope, extend to the Arctic Ocean and empty into the Bering

From above to below:
Shoup Glacier, Prince William Sound. The Nenana River just south of Fairbanks north of the Alaska Range. Great Kobuk Sand Dunes, Kobuk Valley National Park. Boats near village of Akiachak.

Sea or the Cook Inlet. The landscape is divided by these mountain ranges and river systems, which, when crosscut by the arctic and subarctic climate of the region, form innumerable microniches and habitation zones. Overall, though, the two dominant vegetation types are tundra and taiga (boreal forest). As an exception, the extreme southeast part of Alaska, the Southeast Panhandle, is part of the Pacific Northwest Coast, which is dominated by a coastal environment and a temperate rain forest.

While the landscape, ecology and climate vary vastly within Alaska, it can be said that the further north you go, the longer and colder the winters get and the more skill and experience it takes for man to survive in the elements. Structures become important, and it's no surprise that utility has defined modern buildings in the North far more than design. Of course, long before the curious and the settlers were the original inhabitants of the North, who maintained a strong, spiritual and physical connection to the landscape. It was the indigenous people of the North who learned to live in it. They understood survival in the North. More than that, they knew how to thrive and develop rich cultures based on the land and the sea.

Part of survival was knowing how to build a structure that could protect from the elements. These were utilitarian but ingenious structures built from natural materials that provided shelter from rain, wind, snow and predatory animals. Cold is the greatest threat of the arctic. To live in it means to find a way to, at times, escape from it.

Temporary and permanent structures were then one with the earth, whether they were built above and below the ground. The construction of these shelters required an intimate, intelligent understanding of wind forces, snow drifting and other cold climate physics. Dwellings could be ephemeral and transient or permanent, depending on the season and the seasonal activities. The dome-like form of the

From above to below:
Women building an "igloo" with snow blocks, c. 1926. A home in the Yup'ik village of Gambell on St. Lawrence Island, c. 2005. Village of Noatak. Kotzebue.

arctic snow structures offered a minimum exposed surface area and a maximum amount of structural stability. It could warm quickly, stand up to high winds and withstand the weight of a polar bear. When the interior warmth caused the ice to melt, the shape of the dome forced the water to run along the sides of the form and refreeze at the base and strengthening the structural system. As new snow would fall, another level of insulation from the cold was formed. As temperatures increase, the structure simply melts away with no debris left on the land. A more efficient use of materials (and a renewable resource at that) has rarely been seen in the built environment since. Similarly, the early earth houses of semi-nomadic cultures could be temporal or last more than ten years. From a distance the structures looked simply like a small hill. With sod construction, over time the material would meld together and become more solid with age.

The British-Swedish architect Ralph Erskine said that architecture arises as human beings change the landscape. As human beings began to populate the North, they began to change the landscape. As temporary became permanent new ways of living and building had to follow. Erskine encouraged an architecture that eased the contact between indoors and outdoors. He thought buildings should fit well into the land and consider the way climate impacts people.

Vernacular buildings of the modern North have found ways, many inelegant, to deal with snow, icicles, thawing, and freezing. They are functional; they enclose, they protect.

But the North is growing and growing up and with it so is the architecture. Today, with either resident or invited architects creating more and more designs for buildings at latitudes climbing above 60° Fahrenheit (15.6° Centigrade), an opportunity has arisen for a new definition of a northern building – one that is extraordinarily responsive to place and one that is, at the same time, aesthetically provocative. While there

From above to below:
Village of Noatak. Aerial view of landscape near Kotzebue. Village of Akiachak.
Village of Akiachak.

does not seem to be one northern aesthetic to point to – roofs are neither uniformly gabled nor flat, materials are not exclusively natural or manmade – there is a collective knowledge and wisdom that can be defined as northern architecture. It's more than just a building that's constructed in the North – it's northern in the way it responds to the North – the way the architecture mediates the harshness of the low-lying sun without replacing it with the harshness of artificial lights, the way it anticipates snow drifting against the sides, the way it lights up in the darkness, the way it exploits the natural topography and changes the quality of life, and the way it provides visual stimulation in places that sometimes offer little more than a whitescape.

Sometimes it is materiality that ties a building to place – such as Erskine's use of timbers and birch bark in his 1950s Ski Hotel in Borgafjall, Sweden. Other times it is the siting – a form growing out of the landscape so that the landscape itself provides shelter from the cold. Sometimes it is the views out of the building and onto the landscape beyond that reminds the inhabitant and the visitor of where they are and why it is special. While David Chipperfield's design for the Anchorage Museum in Alaska features a glass façade that feels anything but natural to the surrounding environment, it celebrates place in the reflective quality and the new transparency – allowing visitors traveling through exhibitions of the objects of Alaska to look outside to relate those objects to the place they came from.

These are not all new ideas. Even the ancient Greeks employed a building technique the recognized that the winter sun had a low arc in the southern sky, due to the tilt in the Earth at the season, allowing windows in the walls to capture much needed heat from the sun. Therefore, a traditional building is usually built just below the brow of a hill on the southward slope. This way the building is protected by the hill and by surrounding shelterbelts of trees. The north face of the

From above to below:
Downtown Anchorage in winter. Downtown Anchorage in winter with roofline of Alaska Center for the Performing Arts designed by Hardy Holzman Pfeiffer Associates (HHPA). First Avenue in Nome, Alaska, c. 1910. Barracks under construction at Fort Richardson, c. 1949.

building typically has few openings while the south contains the main openings to maximize sun exposure. But old or new, it's the application of these ideas or the decision to reapply the ideas in contemporary design that creates a new North. Early settler societies did not work to imitate the indigenous methods of relating to the environment, including methods of sheltering. They instead focused on the importation of ideas for housing, public buildings and infrastructure. In Alaska, modern society imported notions of architecture, community planning and services from more temperate climates further south. The method of trying to beat the northern climate by building southern structures but with more insulation has not led to better northern living.

Some moments of the 20th century have helped to define Alaska and its buildings, although Alaska's European history began much earlier, with the first European contact in 1741, when Vitus Bering led an expedition for the Russian Navy and returned to Russia from Alaska with sea otter pelts deemed to be the finest fur in the world – prompting fur traders to sail from the shores of Siberia towards the Aleutian Islands. The first European settlement was founded in 1784 and the Russian-American Company began a colonization program during the mid-1800s. In 1867 William H. Seward, the U.S. Secretary of State, negotiated with Russian to purchase Alaska for the U.S. for $7.2 million, prompting Alaska's nickname "Seward's Folly". Alaska was then loosely governed by the militarily and became unofficially a territory of the U.S. In the 1890s, gold rushes in Alaska and nearby Yukon Territory brought thousands of miners and settlers to Alaska and Alaska was granted official territorial status in 1912.

The first major construction project that provided critical infrastructure to the state was the building of the Alaska Railroad in 1915,

From above to below:
Buildings and cars along what was once Fourth Avenue lay in ruins as a result of the tremendous earthquake that rocked Alaska (Anchorage, March 27, 1964). Dr. Ukichiro Nakaya, former professor of physics at Hokkaido, Japan, in one of the cold rooms of the Snow, Ice, and Permafrost Research Establishment at Wilmette, Illinois, c. 1954. Snowmobiles outside village school, Noatak. Quonset hut in ruins, Kodiak Island.

13

which linked north Pacific shipping with tracks that ran from Seward to Interior Alaska via Southcentral Alaska, passing through Anchorage, Fairbanks and other smaller towns that became the "Railbelt". The Railroad was a key player in economic development for the state, moving freight into Alaska while transporting natural resources such as coal and gravel southward.

In 1942, Alaska's building industry faced some of its greatest challenges and opportunities in preparation for the War, designing military bases with aviation fields and hangars and the Alaska Highway.

During World War II, The Aleutians Islands Campaign saw military buildup on the three outer Aleutian Islands – Attu, Agattu and Kiska. The Islands were invaded by Japanese troops and occupied between June 1942 and August 1943. Unalaska/Dutch Harbor became a significant base for the U.S. Army Air Corps and Navy submariners. The U.S. Lend-Lease program involved the flying of American warplanes through Canada to Fairbanks and then Nome; Soviet pilots took possession of these aircraft, ferrying them to fight the German invasion of the Soviet Union. The construction of military bases contributed to the population growth of some Alaskan cities and still provides economic stimulus today.

Statehood did not come until the "last frontier" entered the Union as the 49th state on January 3, 1959. Just five years later, on March 29, 1964, a massive earthquake struck Southcentral Alaska. The "Good Friday Earthquake" killed 131 people and destroyed several villages, mainly as a result of the tsunamis caused by the earthquake. It was the second most powerful earthquake in the recorded history of the world, with a moment magnitude of 9.2; 100 times more powerful than the 1989 San Francisco earthquake. The epicenter was in an unpopulated area; otherwise, thousands more would have been killed. Parts of downtown Anchorage were destroyed and several private

From above to below:
Gracious House Lodge gas station, along Denali Highway. Ten-story cabin north of Anchorage. Gracious House Lodge, along Denali Highway.

homes slid into the Cook Inlet when the earthquake caused the silt-heavy land to quickly erode into the ocean.

This prompted questions about the stability of land for construction growth in Anchorage and Walter J. Hickel, who would later be governor of the state, was one of the only developers willing to take a risk to prove that development of Anchorage's downtown core could continue. His Captain Cook Hotel, built to withstand subsequent earthquakes, still stands as an icon and a testament to his investment in the city today.

In 1975 the first section of pipe was laid for the Trans-Alaska Pipeline, an astounding engineering feat and one of the largest privately-funded and one of the most logistically-complicated projects ever completed in peacetime. It employed tens of thousands of people often in extreme temperatures and conditions and specialized construction techniques were pioneered to build it, as much of the pipeline rests in or on the permafrost.

More than 800 miles (1,287 kilometers) of pipe were laid, eleven pump stations were built and an entire port was constructed to serve oil tankers that transport oil from the pipeline's end. The main construction effort lasted until 1977 and the first barrel of oil was delivered from Prudhoe Bay, Alaska to Valdez, Alaska on July 28, 1988. Sitting 250 miles (402 kilometers) north of the Arctic Circle, 400 miles (644 kilometers) north of Fairbanks and 650 miles (1,046 kilometers) north of Anchorage, the Prudhoe Bay region of Alaska is home to the largest oil field in North America. ARCO and Exxon first discovered oil in the region in March 1968, drilling the Prudhoe Bay State No. 1 well; BP Exploration drilled a confirmation well in 1969. Over the next eight years, the three companies worked to delineate the region and set up an infrastructure, and Prudhoe Bay came "on stream" in June 1977. In

From above to below:
South Anchorage High School, designed by ECI/Hyer, Inc. with Perkins and Will. University of Alaska Museum of the North, Fairbanks, designed by Hammel, Green and Abrahamson collaborating with architect of record GDM of Anchorage, 2007. Conceptual design for Alaska State Capitol in Juneau by Morphosis with mmense Architects, 2005.

1979, production at the field reached a maximum rate of 1.5 million barrels per day. By 2006, more than 10 billion barrels of oil had been produced at Prudhoe Bay. Alaskan architect Edwin Crittenden worked on the design for the Prudhoe Bay infrastructure, creating a building system that sat on top of the frozen tundra with minimal impact and efficient operations.

Oil also meant robust economic times for the state and, through several "boom and bust" cycles, many cities, towns and villages saw their built environment grow dramatically, particularly in Anchorage, which saw several major cultural development projects that define the city's architectural landscape, such as the Alaska Center for the Performing Arts, the Egan Civic and Convention Center, and the expansion of the Anchorage Museum in the 1980s. The trend established early on was to "import" architectural design from outside the state, although the larger firms would be partnered with a local "architect of record".

Architects like Edwin Crittenden, Ralph Alley, Ken Maynard, Charles Bettisworth and others began to develop a local language, however, one that relied on local knowledge of the unique Alaskan environment and its building constraints and challenges and began to forge ahead with architectural styles that were modern and aesthetic as well as meeting the functional needs of the site and client. Many others would come to Alaska and stay, developing practices that began to decrease the "need" for imported expertise. While some worked on large public and corporate projects and established mid- and larger-sized firms to serve the needs of a growing population, others, such as Mike Mense, focused on residential design for the many residents and newcomers in the burgeoning cities. Architecture in rural areas has been proven possible, albeit with tremendous challenges in terms of climate and the accessibility, transport and cost of material. In rural

From above to below:
University of Alaska/Alaska Pacific University Consortium Library, designed by RIM Architects. "Cadillac" by Buck Walsky, Rachelle Dowdy and Dave Cole, temporary installation for the FREEZE project, Anchorage, January, 2009. "Snowball Effect" by Claudia Kappl, temporary installation for the FREEZE project, Anchorage, January, 2009.

Alaska, transportation is not by road but by boardwalks, snow roads, river and air. Small planes and boats are lifelines to communities. Small three- and four-wheel vehicles and snowmachines provide local transportation and the ability to subsist rather than the automobile.

Today it is difficult to claim one architectural "style" for Alaska. The old lingers with the new. Quonset huts remain but have been reappropriated. Residences are constructed out of other massive debris left behind by a frontier lifestyle – airplanes, buses, trailers, boats, water tanks and even an air traffic control tower. There are cabin lifestyles that promote the remote and the temporary, although they are not always low impact. There are materials and language borrowed from the recently established Northwest style even though, it, too, can feel out of place as one moves North. There is urban sprawl, with cookie-cutter housing that does not make any effort to reference place. There is roadside kitch, portable coffee houses, and other structures that define blight or character, depending on your perspective.

Rather than the development of one aesthetic language or form, what is interesting is to watch the continued development of a northern sensibility in architecture – less imported and much more responsive to site and environment. The shared local knowledge of how best to build in the northern climates, as varied as they are within the state, is vast. Rather than importing designs for schools that makes sense in more southern climates, firms like Bettisworth North have been instrumental in developing prototype schools that make sense for Interior Alaska. Their Birch Hill ski lodge in Fairbanks is similarly responsive in terms of providing a contemporary aesthetic within a very site-specific building.

From above to below:
"Snowball Effect" by Claudia Kappl, temporary installation for the FREEZE project, Anchorage, January, 2009. "Expose" by 4LetterWord (Karen Larsen and Mary Ellen Read), temporary installation for the FREEZE project, Anchorage, January, 2009. "Winter Meeting" by Michael Gerace of Black + White Studio Architects and Sonya Kelliher-Combs, temporary installation for the FREEZE project, Anchorage, January, 2009.

Koonce Pfeffer Bettis has worked hard to conquer the logistical challenges of building large schools in remote places, where the seasons are short and the transportation of materials for construction is a feat. International companies with a presence in Alaska have invested in architecture for the residents, such as British Petroleum, which opened its BP Energy Center in 2002, designed by Bruce Williams of Koonce Pfeffer Bettis to reflect both its purpose as a center for nonprofits and its location within the wooded but urban core.

Architects from outside the state are now tasked with designing buildings within the state that add something to the local aesthetic and the ideas of northern buildings. David Chipperfield was chosen as the design architect for the new wing of the Anchorage Museum, working with Kumin Associates of Anchorage as the architect of record, and the driver in his design was a building that would reference the landscape that surrounds the city and that would connect the objects in the Museum to the place they represent. Joan Soranno and the GDM/HGA architectural team designed the expansion to the Museum of the North on the University of Alaska campus in Fairbanks to convey a sense of Alaska, with innovative lines and spaces evoking images of alpine ridges, glaciers, breakup on the Yukon River, and the aurora.

Morphosis was part of a national competition to design a new state Capitol building in Juneau. Conceived as a gift framed by its majestic Juneau site, the selection committee wanted the Capitol building to communicate to this and future generations what it is to be uniquely Alaskan. The building was intended to synthesize iconic and contemporary elements to provide Alaska with a celebrated landmark and destination. Building upon the architectural legacy of Ameri-

From above to below:
"Winter Meeting" by Michael Gerace of Black + White Studio Architects and Sonya Kelliher-Combs, temporary installation for the FREEZE project, Anchorage, January, 2009. "Northern Sky Circle" by molo, temporary installation for FREEZE project, Anchorage, 2009. Campfire inside "Northern Sky Circle" by molo, temporary installation for FREEZE project, Anchorage, 2009. Walls of labyrinth, "Northern Sky Circle" by molo, temporary installation for FREEZE project, Anchorage, 2009.

can Capitols, the Morphosis design, developed in partnership with mmenseArchitects, proposed a contemporary interpretation of the statehouse, in its organization and forms and through its most recognizable icon, the dome. Their Capitol, had the project gone forward (politics, as they so often do, got in the way), would have transformed Juneau's skyline and provided a unifying symbol for Alaska that exuded confidence, transparency and accessibility.

Often some of the most thoughtful architecture can be found in the residential neighborhoods, down winding gravel streets that go up mountainsides or sit quietly within or at the edges of downtowns. Here experimentation is at its height and materiality and light are explored at a more intimate and personal level, examining what it really means to inhabit the North on a daily basis, both day and night, summer and winter.

Other ways of looking at the North through architecture and design are being explored, outside of the realm of building construction. In January 2009, the Alaska Design Forum, International Gallery of Contemporary Art and Anchorage Museum partnered to present FREEZE, an international exhibition of outdoor installations highlighting northern elements – snow, ice and light. Architects, artists and designers from around the world such as Studio Granda of Iceland, Christoph Kapeller of CK Architecture with Buro Happold and Lita Albuquerque of Los Angeles, Future Farmers of San Francisco, molo, Kobayashi + Zedda and Ana Rewakowicz of Canada, Claudia Kappl of Arizona, and others worked alongside Alaskan architects and designers in downtown Anchorage in temperatures dipping to -25° Fahrenheit (-31.7° Centigrade), some of the lowest on record. The designers battled the subarctic extremes, becoming scientists, inventors, sculptors and constructors and created 14 unique and temporal

From above to below:
Firewood stacked outside entrance to "Northern Sky Circle" by molo, temporary installation for FREEZE project, Anchorage, 2009. Visitors on the Delaney Park Strip in downtown Anchorage viewing temporary installations as part of the FREEZE project, 2009. "Ice Fracture" by Ana Rewakowicz and Kobayashi + Zedda Architects, temporary installation for FREEZE project, Anchorage, 2009. "Sound Mirror" by mayer sattler-smith and Marisa Favretto, temporary installation for FREEZE project, Anchorage, 2009.

experiences that invited interaction through movement, sight and sound. Cars were sunk, scuba divers were called, forklifts were used to raise 205,000 pounds (92,985 kilograms) of ice, snow was trucked in, labyrinths were formed, tunnels were dug, traffic cones and frozen heads were cast, and candles were lit at a fragile 99-foot (30 meters) table constructed over ten days. While thousands of visitors walked between, crawled on and circled through the installations, within a week of the public opening, the temperatures had shifted by more than 60° Fahrenheit (15.5° Centigrade) and FREEZE began to melt. Snow changed color, ice became transparent, and some visions slipped away. The impermanence of the works paralleled the fleeting, ephemeral qualities of winter, and the uncontrollability of nature.

The projects featured in this publication represent more than structures in the North. They represent an architecture that responds to cold, natural light and extreme conditions and is site-specific in its conception. These are not transplanted designs, but an approach to understand and celebrate the unique qualities of the northern latitudes. They offer a way of living in the North that does not isolate man from environment but unites the North with the northerner. The stories told by these projects combine isolation with city life, lightness with darkness, tradition with innovation, urbanity with the ultimate grandeur of nature. These buildings contribute significantly to the architectural landscape and the rediscovery of the Alaska. As the northern climate changes, so does the approach with which we inhabit it.

From above to below:
Detail of "Sound Mirror" by mayer sattler-smith and Marisa Favretto, temporary installation for FREEZE project, Anchorage, 2009. Village of Deering on the Northeast coast of the Seward Peninsula, Kotzebue Sound. Denali National Park (Mount McKinley).

CONCEIVING AN ALASKAN TRADITION:
Listening to the Voices of Landscape and Culture
by Juhani Pallasmaa

"In the fusion of place and soul, the soul is as much of a container of place as place is a container of soul, and both are susceptible to the same forces of destruction."[1]

Alaska is a land of immense scale and sublime natural beauty. A visitor is immediately stunned by the majestic formations of land, water and ice, and the extraordinary freshness of the air. When thinking of Alaska, images of land rather than people, wildernesses rather than towns, landscapes rather than buildings, nature rather than human culture, arise in one's mind. Everywhere, including the city of Anchorage, one feels like being at an edge, a fragile boundary line between civilization and untamed nature, and one senses the infiniteness beyond this experiential borderline. Even in the very center of any Alaskan town one is aware of the immensity of the surrounding void of nature.

I have experienced places that have reminded me of the totality of the world, and in these locations I have sensed the enormous mass of the earth and the curvature of its surface beneath my feet. This sensation of the continuity and immensity of the earth is evoked in the middle of oceans, the great sand deserts, and the all-white expanses of snow above the tree line in the North. This feeling of a seamless continuum and togetherness of things can also be felt in the mountain landscapes where the imagined echo of the tremors of the earth's crust carries one's fantasy to landscapes beyond what is actually perceived.

From above to below:
Fireweed in bloom. Winter view of downtown Anchorage from the west, Chugach Mountains behind. View from Seward.

Landscapes also mold and mediate our understanding of time; they concretize the rhythms and cycles beyond those of pressured daily life from geological time to the cycle of seasons and days. Landscapes make us experience the slow and patient time of the physical world. This cyclic time of perpetual return and repetition is calming and therapeutic. Alaskan landscapes convey a silencing sense of endless time and the transitoriness of human culture. The rich wild life reminds one of the paradisaic beginnings of the world.

In Alaska, landscape and nature always dominate culture; any human structure appears temporary and fragile against the eternity of the landscape. These settings are surely a great challenge for architecture, an inspiration and responsibility at the same. It must feel simultaneously a privilege and a humbling task to make one's trace on the face of these majestic and virgin settings. Yet, this is what man needs to do; we need to mark and establish our presence in the world, give a human scale to scalelessness, turn immensity into a place, and give endless time its human measure.

The Alaskan landscape calls for combined sensitivity and strength, humility and pride. The age-old indigenous traditions produced impressively ingenious architectural structures and artifacts utilizing the scarcely available materials and other resources. Alaskan traditional constructions often marked the extreme edge of human survival. The most impressive and unarguable beauty of human artifacts usually arises from the logic of necessity and scarcity of means rather than abundance and unlimited choice and freedom. As a consequence of such utter limitations, Inupiat cultures, for instance, have produced artifacts that are as impressive in their ingenious functionality and inventive use of materials, and as pleasing in their shapes and details as any artifacts in human history. The early architectures of the Russian era as well as the constructions of the early American settlers reflect imported traditions but they are also finely adapted to the local conditions and limitations.

From above to below:
Arctic cotton. Winter landscape near Eureka. A former Inupiat home along the Arctic coast, in the eastern Arctic National Wildlife Refuge.

Today's architect and designer, conscious and respectful of the local traditions, faces the chasm that separates traditional constructions, objects and technologies from our contemporary technologized omnipotence. Traditional technologies were "weak" enough to permit specific local situations to impact the built form. Today's technologies are all too powerful and they have an unavoidable universalizing and leveling off effect. Similarity and sameness replaces differentiation and uniqueness.

How to project a sense of cultural tradition and continuity in functions, technologies and scales that never existed in history before our time? How to create a sense of cultural continuity and rootedness? In areas where urban cultures have accumulated gradually during millennia, such as the historical urban areas of Europe, the yarn of culture is usually clearly visible and readable, whereas any culture in which construction changes from an indigenous local tradition directly into a modern or post-modern phase, encounters deep difficulties in grasping and perpetuating a sense of identity. Yet, the preservation and mediation of a sense of cultural continuity and tradition is a fundamental value of human settings; we are historical beings and we cannot dwell in a placeless space or in detached moments of time. Our desire is to live in experientially distinct places and in a mental continuum of cultural time.

T. S. Eliot, the poet, points out the value of tradition as well as the difficulties of grasping and maintaining it; he writes about literature, of course, but his views are directly applicable in architecture. "Tradition is a matter of much wider significance. It cannot be inherited, and if you want it you must obtain it by great labor. It involves, in the first place, the historical sense […] and the historical sense involves a perception, not only of the pastness of the past, but of its presence; the historical sense compels a man to write [or, to design] not merely with his own generation in his bones, but with a feeling that the

From above to below:
A view of the Inupiat village of Kaktovik from the frozen pack ice on the Arctic Ocean. Homes stand in the Yup'ik village of Gambell on St. Lawrence Island, c. 2005. Dutch Harbor.

whole of the literature [architecture] … has a simultaneous existence and composes a simultaneous order."[2]

I personally faced the problem of mediating and expressing a sense of tradition when designing the Sámi Lapp Museum in Finnish Lapland 15 years ago. Lapp culture and life-style still exist, although in a dramatically modernized way, but Sámi culture never produced museums, or physical structures of the scale of our projects, not to speak of the incorporation of today's technologies and materials. There is no "traditional" Sámi architecture of museums or public buildings. Consequently, the architectural concept had to be based on a "historical sense", an understanding of the historicity of life, culture and things, as the master poet suggests above. In architecture this implies that things appear rooted instead of invented, layered in meaning rather than unidimensional and formalistic, timeless rather than fashion conscious. In short, my task as the architect called paradoxically for the creation of a sense of traditionality instead of following or interpreting existing structures or themes of the actual past. Such a task is, of course, a tightrope walk between interpretation and fabrication, authenticity and falsehood. Altogether, today's aspirations for regionally adapted architecture have the great danger of falling into the trap of manipulated imagery and calculated thematicization. As Eliot argues, a tradition is not a thing that can be possessed, it "must be obtained by great labor", i.e. the sense of regional and cultural specificity has to be achieved through "poetic chemistry", to use a notion of Gaston Bachelard[3]. In my view, the complexity of culture is always beyond description and thematicization; culture cannot be imitated or invented, it has to be authentically experienced and lived.

In the Alaskan context, real landscapes with their specific dynamics, scales, directionalities, moods, etc., provide a solid starting point, the horizon line as it were, for any localized architectural ideas. The sense of cultural rootedness, however, must arise from the author's personal sensitivity to the historicity of culture, or human life at large, and the re-interpretation of the combined assurance and modesty by which the historical dwellers of the region occupied their land and left their marks on it. There is no historical Alaskan architecture that could directly be transferred to today's construction, except for a general respect for the land and its richnesses. An Alaskan tradition needs to be conceived by culturally and artistically sensitive individuals.

Regrettably, the realities of today's construction tend to go heavily against the grain of localized and culture-specific expressions. As Milan Kundera argues, the well-to-do western consumer and mass-media culture is doomed to settings of kitsch: "The aesthetics of mass media are by necessity the aesthetics of kitsch; as the mass media gradually extend and penetrate into every aspect of our life, kitsch becomes our everyday aesthetics and morality. Only some time ago Modernism implied a non-conformist rebellion against received thought and kitsch. Nowadays Modernity blends into the immense vitality of mass media and to be modern means a fierce attempt to keep up with time and adapt, to be even more adaptive than the most adaptive. Modernity has pulled the robe of kitsch on its shoulders."[4] The writer's verdict may sound discouraging and hopeless, but it is unarguable that the forceful logic of technologized construction, globalization of economies and materials, as well as the currently universal ideals and fashions in design, aggressively distributed by media, all tend to eliminate the possibility of an architecture rooted in the specificity of place. It is exactly the severity of the current cultural condition that makes the striving for authenticity in architecture and the arts so significant for our future existential reality. In my view, it would be wiser for architects today to listen to the voice of the land they are building on more keenly than to scan international architectural journals. Perhaps, we should rather try to understand who we are than aspire for what we desire to become.

The urgency of the escalating ecological problems and the consequent call for sustainable architecture, clearly provide an essential strand of thinking and action to re-unite architecture with its location and to strengthen the identity of place. When taken seriously, the ecological imperative will replace the sentimentality and visual pictoresqueness about local identity with a new realism of geography, climate, economy, technology as well as local culture. There was no sentimentality in traditional cultures as they were obliged to follow the logic of survival; sentimentality only arises through excessive and uncritical freedom of choice.

As the R. P. Harrison quote in the beginning of my essay suggests, place and mind, the external physical world and the inner mental world are intertwined. Indeed, as I occupy a landscape, the landscape dwells in me. As Amos Rapoport convincingly argues in his classic book House Form and Culture[5], architecture has never and nowhere been a direct reflection of given physical and material conditions, as architecture is always primarily a cultural expression and determined by cultural choices and aspirations.

When building physical settings for our practical activities, we both reflect images of our mental lives and we structure and condition them. As we build our houses, we also construct our mental world. We live in mental images as much as in material houses. Rainer Maria Rilke, another master poet, uses the beautiful notion Weltinnenraum[6], the inner space of the world, in reference to our mental and lived space that is not only a projection or an internalization of the external physical space; it co-exists and is chiasmatically bound with the material world. The experience of placeness is seminal for our capacity to dwell; it is mentally impossible to dwell in a placeless space. It is the task of architecture to create the ingredients of this experience of place that arises from both the geographic and cultural realities. Teilhard de Chardin writes about a mysterious "Omega Point"[7], from which the world appears complete and correct. It is the duty of architecture, in each design task, to create this mystical point for the purpose of structuring and articulating individual and collective experience of the world, culture and life.

The recent Alaskan projects selected for this book exemplify various architectural strategies suspended between the polarities of universal technological rationalism and the search for a localized identity and specificity of place. The projects are also serious attempts to create a contemporary architectural authenticity in Alaska, whose construction in the past decades has regrettably, in most cases, been dominated by cultural carelessness and mediocrity.

In most of these projects, the desire to follow today's universal architectural expressions is stronger than the interest to be specifically rooted in Alaskan geographic and cultural soil. The universalizing impact of today's technological, media, and consumer culture is so forceful that even countries that have been known globally, since the beginning of the modern era, for their recognizable design cultures, such as the Netherlands, Denmark, Finland and Japan, have lost much of their design identity during the past two decades.

It is perhaps also fair to make the observation that the selected Alaskan projects tend to react more clearly and poetically to their immediate landscapes and urban environments than resonate with the larger Alaskan landscape or cultural identity. The subtle dialogue of the BP Energy Center in Anchorage, for instance, placed in a dense birch thicket, demonstrates well this poetic weaving of architecture into its immediate setting; even the system of narrow window slits derives from the visual pattern of birch bark, whereas the light green color used in the building derives from the coloration of young birch leaves. Regardless of its conceptual strength and contextual subtlety, it would not be easy, however, to identify it as a specifically Alaskan project on the basis of mere photographs.

The selected private residences are also in a refined interplay with their landscape contexts. The Phelps/Burke, Buser/Chapoton and Nearpoint residences derive their dynamics from their sloping sites, and the impressive distant views, in relation to which the various functions and spatial layouts are organized.

The Phelps/Burke residence by mayer sattler-smith is a narrow, rectangular structure set perpendicular to the sloping site. The living room – dining – kitchen functions are placed on the upper floor culminating in a large glass wall and terrace, opening to a mesmerizing view. An elegantly conceived stair leads to the lower floor with bedroom and individual office rooms, whereas a vertical two-story studio space located on the opposite side of an outdoor corridor reconnects the two floors. The industrial materials make the building read as a rationally conceived and executed artifact rather than being embedded in the landscape.

The Buser/Chapoton residence by mayer sattler-smith in Big Lake, located at the highest point of a hill, dominates an impressive panoramic sweep of mostly untouched landscape. Again, the rooms are organized in relation to the view, and a large roof terrace provides a completely uninterrupted vista of the spectacular setting. The house itself intentionally reads as a detached object set in the landscape, underlining thus the contrast between wilderness and human life. The house is a refuge and a prospect, a point of departure and return.

The Nearpoint residence designed by Steve Bull of Workshop for Architecture and Design also occupies a high point on a hillside mediating between the tactile intimacy of the forest around and the distant visual landscape. South light penetrates through the spaces giving a sense of vitality and warmth. The house is functionally subdivided into three separate units. The client's practice of Buddhism is reflected in the special ambience of the separate tatami room. The house is well detailed and crafted, and the material palette (rough-sawn cedar, polished concrete, wood block floor and bamboo details) gives a combined sense of moderateness and luxury.

The small addition to the Davis residence on 23rd Street near downtown Anchorage, by Black + White Studio Architects, is skillfully and tightly woven into its suburban setting, around and within an existing ordinary house. The project creates a rich and cozy interplay between old and new, between spaces, materials, colors and light. The architectural intervention and elaboration is relaxed and inspired, respectful and inventive, at the same time. The inside and outdoor spaces, sunken courts, structures, materials, transparencies and translucencies, are carefully articulated to create a sense of a rich microcosm that is decisively richer than the image of a mere suburban house. The skylight above the dining table is mirrored to reflect the sky and an adjacent tree in order to evoke the ambience of dining outdoors underneath a tree. The project has been largely built by the occupants themselves using recycled materials and this fact surely adds to the feeling of rootedness and the real.

The Maasen/Gowens residence on its hillside site in Anchorage by Black + White Studio Architects creates a village-like cluster of volumes, courtyards and corridors, partly sunk into the slope. Living room – kitchen – dining, a two story bedroom volume, a guest room with an office above and a separate garage are the four volumetric units of the "village"; the clearstory above the kitchen area adds to the volumetric rhythm. The roof of the largest volume serves as a garden roof terrace. As in the other projects of the office, the spatial interplay is richly and precisely articulated. The subdivision of the program into separate units, semi-individual houses, as it were, provides an exceptional sense of privacy and solitude.

The sectional solution creates different experiences of floor levels; the first floor level reads as terraced ground on the hillside, whereas the master bedroom is an elevated floor, the guest room a cave of sorts, and the office above, with a separate entry from outdoors, appears as an attic floor. The basic sectional dynamics provides distinct views and a sense of prospect through nearly fully glazed walls, whereas the sunken entry courtyard and the retaining wall against the slope provide a sense of directionality and protection. The material palette is well-considered and elegant.

The Homer Public Library, designed by ECI/Hyer and located in the picturesque coastal town of Homer, exemplifies today's striving for sustainable public buildings (the project received a LEED®-Silver Certificate) connected architecturally and socially to its natural and cultural landscape. The architectural language is a blend of technological pragmatism and rural Alaskan rusticity in the choice of methods of construction, materials and detailing. The selected materials and artworks are also motivated by the desire to support local industries, crafts and artists. An abstracted landscaping ties the building to its semi-urban vicinity. The main library space with its heavy roof structures and visible ductwork creates the ambience of a workshop that positively lowers the psychological threshold of library as a cultural institute. The rough matter-of-factness of materials and details creates a relaxed mood that resonates with traditional constructions of this small and idyllic harbor town and turns the library into a collectively shared living space of the community.

By Alaskan law, every child is entitled to equal education. This principle of democratic education makes it necessary to construct school buildings even under most demanding conditions. The system of rural village schools, one in Kotlik and three in the Yup'ik area, designed by KPB Architects, is a result of exceptionally serious design conditions, and constraints. The structures are located in an area of permafrost, heavy snowfall, -22° Fahrenheit (-30° Centigrade), and winds that can reach the crueling velocity of 120 miles per hour (193 kilometer per hour). All materials and equipment for construction have to be transported by barges from the south, and as no technical expertise exists in the village after the construction workers have left the finished work, all structural and technical choices have to be based on high reliability and low maintenance. Due to the permafrost as well as high snow drifts formed by wind, the structures are built on piles and elevated decks. In addition to the severe technical parameters, the projects also needed to be administratively and psychologically skillfully managed through series of negotiations with the village elders. The architectural language deliberately and appropriately reflects today's industrialized construction practices, whereas cultural and behavioral traditions of the users have been incorporated in the spatial solutions.

The Ravenwood Veterinary Clinic by mayer sattler-smith located in Eagle River is an elegant rational composition with a rectangular overall shape, partial second-floor volume and roof deck; the lower floor volume with a dark corrugated metal façade creates a pedestal for the wood-faced upper floor with a horizontally emphasized roof which creates a counterpoint to the black base. The external walls are rather closed, defining a boundary, whereas the interior spaces within the enclosing perimeter wall are abundantly glazed creating a sense of spatial flow. The clinic is entered through a small enclosed courtyard (the perforated metal profiles of the wall section that encloses the courtyard either create the sense of opening or enclosure

depending on the viewing angle) and the overall ambience is comfortingly welcoming and domestic. The interiors are well-proportioned and detailed with color accent – the red floor of the operation rooms creates a sense of significance and drama. The building is related with its context through its appropriate scale, whereas through its reductive geometry it introduces a dialogue with the buildings of the town and the distant mountain silhouette.

The expansion of the Anchorage Museum by David Chipperfield is more conceptually grounded than the projects by local architects. The project combines a rigorously articulated and modulated functional, structural and technical scheme with an abstracted and distanced imagery of ice, snow, water and sky suggested by the specially manufactured, partly reflective 3-layer glass panes of the façades. The Museum echoes a mental image of Alaskan landscape and climate rather than any immediate or real context; in fact, the building with the future planted grove, creates its own autonomous context, a self-sufficient oasis or paradise of sorts. The entity paradoxically evokes an image of mythical Alaskan wilds in the very center of the largest city of the state. The external image that hides the interiors and effectively reflects and fragments the urban setting, creates a curious and forceful sense of immense distance, solitude, and void, that invokes a conceptualized image of the Alaskan geographic condition.

NOTES
1 Robert Pogue Harrison, "Sympathetic Miracles", Gardens: An Essay on the Human Condition. The University of Chicago Press, Chicago and London, 2008, p. 130.
2 T. S. Eliot, "Tradition and Individual Talent", Selected Essays. Faber and Faber, London, 1999, p. 14.
3 Gaston Bachelard, Water and Dreams: An Essay on the Imagination of Matter. The Pegasus Foundation, Dallas, Texas, 1983, p. 46.
4 Milan Kundera, Romaanin taide [The Art of the Novel]. Werner Söderström Oy, Helsinki, 1986, p. 165. Translation by Juhani Pallasmaa.
5 Amos Rapoport, House Form and Culture. University of Wisconsin, Milwaukee, 1969.
6 Liisa Ehnwald, editor, "Lukijalle" [To the reader]. Rainer Maria Rilke, Hiljainen taiteen sisin; kirjeitä vuosilta 1900–1926. [The silent core of art; letters 1900–1926], TAI-teos, Helsinki, 1997, p. 8.
7 See, Pierre Teilhard de Chardin, The Phenomenon of Man. HarperCollins Publishers, New York.

NEARPOINT RESIDENCE

ANCHORAGE, ALASKA / 2009

Located in Southcentral Alaska in a wide valley, Anchorage is bordered on the west, north, and south by Knik Arm and Turnagain Arm of Cook Inlet. The Chugach Mountains to the east have a general elevation of 4,000 to 5,000 feet (1,219–1,524 meters), with peaks from 8,000 to 10,000 feet (2,438–3,048 meters). These mountains block warm air from the Gulf of Mexico, keeping precipitation relatively low. The Alaska Range to the north protects the city from cold air from the state's interior; thus temperatures in Anchorage are usually 25 to 30° Fahrenheit (-3.9 to 0° Centigrade) warmer than temperatures in the rest of the state. While the area has four seasons, their length and characteristics differ from those of the middle latitudes; snows arrive in October and leave in mid-April, while annual average snowfall is seventy inches. Daylight hours vary from 19 in late June to 6 hours in late December.

Situated on a short ridge at the base of the Chugach Mountains, the Nearpoint residence offers expansive views of the Alaska Range to the north, and downtown Anchorage and the Cook Inlet to the west. A clearing made for an unrealized house that had been previously planned for the property provided a natural location for this private home in a birch grove. Workshop for Architecture and Design focused on four primary design concerns: creating specific landscape and social relationships that would be transformed as the occupants inhabit different areas of the home and site; direct access to landscape and exterior spaces; exploration of the differing relationship between use and thermal performance; and environmental responsibility. At the beginning of the design phase, the client sent a postcard to Workshop for Architecture and Design with a short list of values to be embodied in the house, which included energy and environmental responsibility, timeless and durable construction, ability to house an eclectic mix of art and collections, respect for nature, sense of community, simplicity, and a creative use of space. The architects responded by creating a clean interior volume with open living spaces that share in all communal activity. Private spaces within the home are modest, bringing the emphasis back to the shared spaces and family life. Disturbance of the exterior site was minimal, and the landscape is a dominant feature of the home. By orienting the house horizontally along the site's ridge, the architects ensured that the structure relates to the forest understory as well as to the broad panorama beyond. Interior elements like the use of wide, high windows coupled with low horizontal ones emphasize this scope of magnification. In this way, the house extends along the ridge like a path with views and connections to both the near and distant landscapes, grounding the owners to the foliage and topography of the site as well as the vast wilderness around it.

View from west with Chugach Range as backdrop.

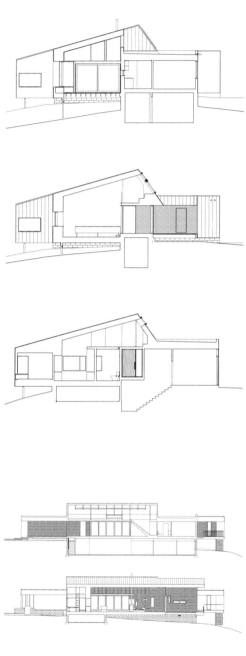

From above to below, from left to right:
West-facing façade. Elevations. Building sections. View of hallway to bedrooms and entrance to main living area.

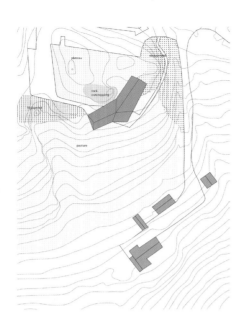

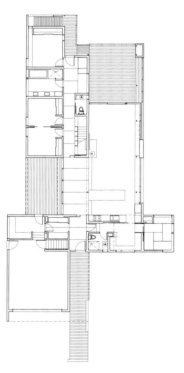

From above to below, from left to right:
Site plan. Floor plan. Main living area.

BP ENERGY CENTER

ANCHORAGE, ALASKA / 2002

Alaska has vast energy resources. Major oil and gas reserves are found in the Alaska North Slope and Cook Inlet basins. Alaska ranks second in the nation in crude oil production. Prudhoe Bay on Alaska's North Slope is the highest yielding oil field in the United States and on North America, typically producing about 400,000 barrels per day. The Trans-Alaska Pipeline can pump up to 2.1 million barrels of crude oil per day, more than any other crude oil pipeline in the United States. The oil and gas industry dominates the Alaskan economy, with more than 80% of the state's revenues derived from petroleum extraction. BP is one of the leading oil and gas production and exploration companies in the state.

Tucked in a small wooded area in the shadow of BP Exploration's Alaska headquarters in Anchorage, the BP Energy Center offers a secluded, cozy space for conferences, meetings, and events for the state's non-profit organizations. Before construction the site was a swampy area populated by birch trees next to one of the city's two main highways, and was in sharp contrast to the tidy look of the huge, manicured lawns of the nearby high-rise.

While sketching and painting the setting on site, the lead designer of the project, Bruce Williams of Koonce Pfeffer Bettis, discovered a drainage ditch covered in an area of new grass and bushes that was once Blueberry Lake. The idea of nature reclaiming itself from humankind's industrial footprint inspired him and led him to the decision to place the building at the edge of the forest away from the highway – the visitors would walk east, away from the parking lot, through birch trees, to arrive at the center. The noise level diminishes with each step through the woodland; as a result, the center has a retreatlike quality enhanced by the building itself. The foliage of birch trees obscures the view of the building from the main parking area and street during the summer. But in the winter the view through the leafless trees reveals a modern building clad in metal, with a two-story southern wing in a box form clad in panels of opaque green spandrel glass that echo the color of the birch leaves that sprout during the first two weeks of spring. The color of the building and the color of the leaves synchronize for a moment in time every year.

A form cantilevers out into the forest canopy, and windows punched through the façade provide a framed view of the birch forest – a perspective meant to stimulate contemplation rather than to distract. The patterns of Alaskan birch bark inspired the long, thin, horizontal windows. The 13,500-square-foot (1,254-square-meters) center offers opportunities to learn more about the energy industry through interpretive displays integrated into the facility's design. The two-story complex includes three pods, one large meeting space to the south, an exhibit space to the north, and a second

Glass façade, southeast corner.

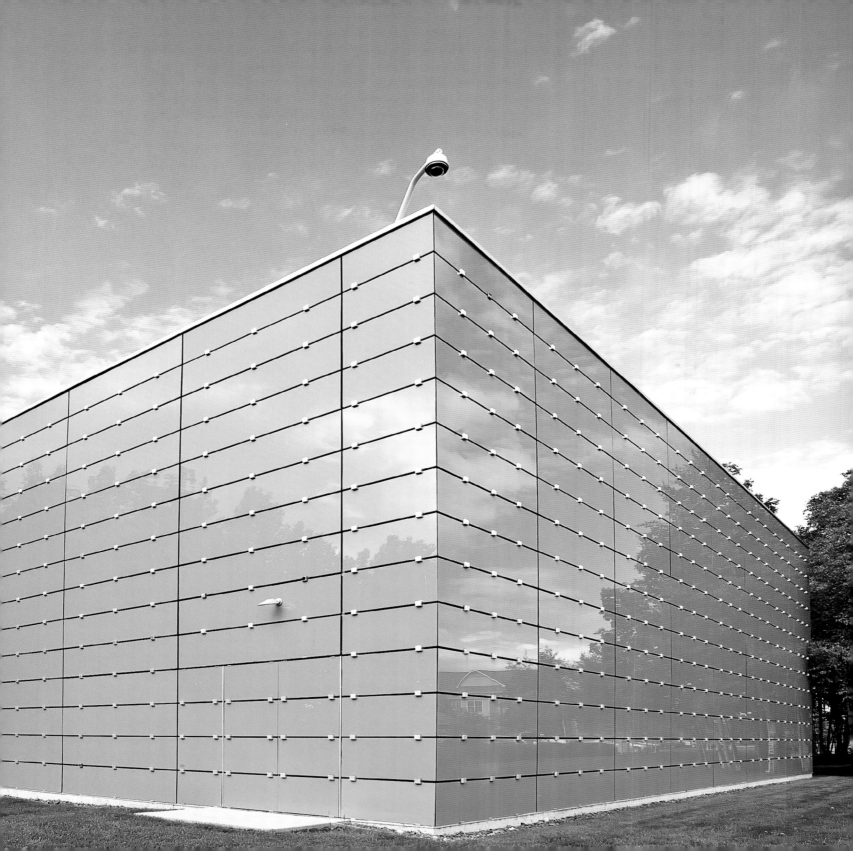

floor with several smaller meeting spaces. The ground-floor pods are connected by glass corridors that also serve as exhibit spaces. The center's six meeting/conference spaces can hold anywhere from 20 to 100 people each. One room provides a nonconventional, living-room style space designed for informal strategic planning. Other small spaces for minimeetings are located throughout the building. An internal "pathway" ties the facility together, with small interpretive exhibits that highlight the role of energy in the Alaskan economy and culture.

The primary art installation involves a "story pipeline" in which a cross section of Alaskans tell their stories about living in the state through videotaped interviews that are played on an LCD screen that sends the words along an LCD ribbon that moves down the exhibit hall, through the glass out to the exterior site, and into the woods like a stream of words and red light winding through the forest.

From above to below, from left to right:
East façade. Detail, northwest façade. Interior entry. Detail, glass façade.

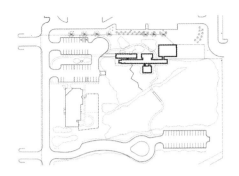

From above to below, from left to right:
Glass façade, southeast corner. Site plan. Floor plan.
Elevations. Approach to east entrance.

ANCHORAGE MUSEUM AT RASMUSON CENTER, NEW WING

ANCHORAGE, ALASKA / 2009

Anchorage is Alaska's only true metropolis. With a population exceeding a quarter of a million, Anchorage is home to almost half the people in Alaska. It is the only Alaskan city with a real skyline, although even the tallest buildings are dwarfed by the mountainscape that serves as the city's backdrop. The Chugach are to the east of the city. To the north is the Alaska Range, which rises to 20,320 feet (6,193 meters) at the peak of Mount McKinley, the tallest mountain in North America. On a clear day the peak of McKinley is visible even from downtown Anchorage some 130 miles away (209 kilometers). To the west of the city lies Cook Inlet, named for Captain James Cook, the British explorer who sailed to Alaska in 1778. The drive along Cook Inlet is one of the most scenic in Alaska, and this part of the inlet (known as Turnagain Arm) experiences the second-greatest tidal variation in North America – only the one at Nova Scotia's Bay of Fundy is greater.

The ambitious 80,000-square-foot (7,432-square-meter) expansion of the Anchorage Museum at Rasmuson Center by architect David Chipperfield responded to the shortcomings of the existing building, which was built in the era of museums that did not have views in or out, and which had a main entrance that faced away from the heart of the rest of the downtown, and also responded to the city's setting. His design provided a new main entrance facing west and a unique façade composed of insulated fritted glass striped with mirrored glass that re-flects the sky and surrounding mountains. The constantly changing surface "takes on the light qualities that are here", said Chipperfield. "One of the great materials of Alaska is the light." The glazing and pattern were designed specifically to meet the challenges of the extreme environment: allowing natural light in while minimizing the glare from the low angle of the northern sun, and resisting condensation that comes with temperature swings and precipitation. The glass panels were preassembled prior to shipping for easy installation and, as the skin of the new addition, contrast overtly with the original building's brick-clad exterior.

A public plaza links the museum with the downtown area through a birch-tree forest planted inside a two-acre sanctuary that offers open-air spaces for nature exploration, quiet reflection, outdoor activities, and a permanent sculpture by British artist Antony Gormley. The more than 604-foot-wide glass panels that make up the façade allow an interchange between the outside and inside. Transparent sections of glass allow views inside the building, while transluscent sections allow for reflection. Natural light enhances the experience of the visitor when traveling through the building's interior, preventing the "museum fatigue" that can come from closed-in, darkened spaces. This use of light deliberately contrasts with antiquated notions of museums as dark boxes with the sole purpose of protecting the objects inside. Chipperfield took advantage of new technologies

Façade detail.

in UV protection – which allow for transparency without compromising protection from ultraviolet rays – to incorporate natural light, which in turn influences individual interior spaces made distinct through different colors and materials. At the same time, the four-story building promises dramatic views that drive gallery organization and traffic flow. The flow is vertical: visitors head to temporary exhibits by climbing a large, metal staircase that adds a sculptural element to the interior. Third floor galleries feature a view of downtown Anchorage and the Alaska Range, while the fourth-floor gallery offers a unique reward – an expansive view of the Chugach Foothills as a backdrop to the city. To contrast with the cool temperatures outside, Chipperfield used a palette of warm colors and natural materials in the interior to provide a sense of welcome as visitors enter the building. The first-floor public spaces differ starkly from the neutrality of the glass and the cool blue of the sky and surrounding mountains. The entry lobby features bright yellow metal panels between concrete columns, to form walls, and a bright yellow fiberglass front desk. The cafe, just off the main entrance, is deep red, and the towering walls surrounding the main staircase are clad with wood panels. The exhibition galleries return the building to a subtle palette, with charcoal gray floors of poured concrete and the repeating forms of concrete columns.

From above to below, from left to right:
Main entry. Fourth-floor gallery. West façade. North façade.

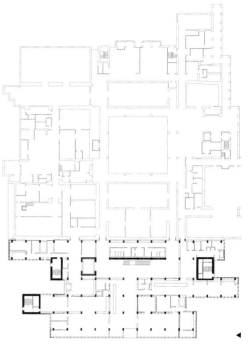

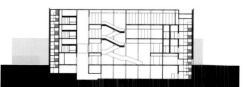

From above to below, from left to right:
Glass façade. Floor plan. Building section. Southwest
corner of façade.

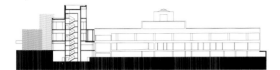

From above to below, from left to right:
Building sections. Workers construct façade, with
Chugach Range beyond.

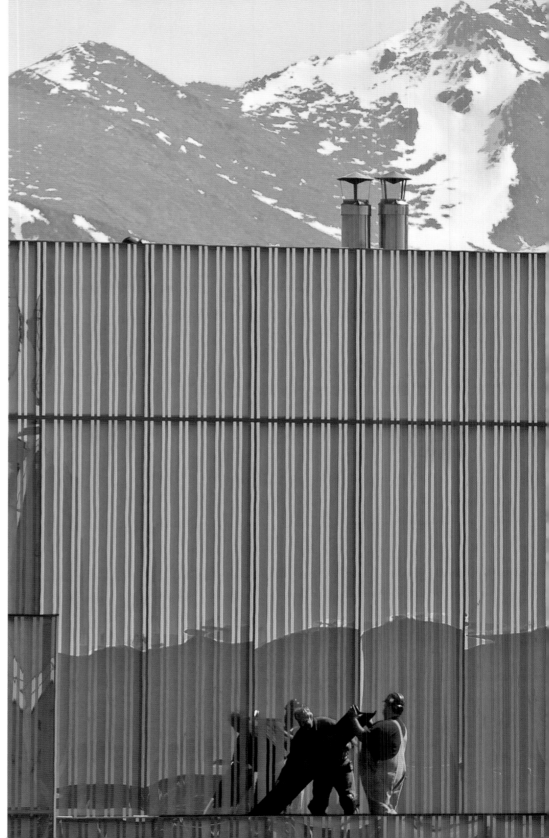

BUSER/CHAPOTON RESIDENCE

BIG LAKE, ALASKA / 2009

The community of Big Lake, Alaska, sits along the shore of Big Lake, a boating and fishing recreation area that is extremely popular during summer months. With a population of about 2,700 the community is west of Wasilla off the Parks Highway in the Matanuska-Susitna Borough. Big Lake residents were hit by Alaska's most destructive wildfire in June 1996. It destroyed more than 400 structures in the Big Lake and Houston areas and burned about 37,000 acres (14,973 hectares). Still, numerous Anchorage residents own vacation and weekend homes there.

The Buser/Chapoton residence sits on glacial marine sediment (a type of clay that occurs in high latitudes), tilted toward Mount McKinley in the Alaska Range. The 2,500-square-foot (232-square-meter) house sits on 20 acres and faces unoccupied land to the west, intensifying the sense of isolation and wilderness. Situated on the highest point of a hill, the house dominates an impressive panoramic sweep of mostly untouched landscape, with mountains rising at every horizon line.

The residence also overlooks the site of an old house that survived the devastating wildfire. The owner of the house, dog musher Martin Buser, four-time Iditarod winner, saved his home from the flames of the forest fire as it was cutting a swath of destruction across the valley and forcing an area-wide evacuation. Buser stayed at his home throughout the fire, dousing the land and the home with water. Still, Buser and his wife eventually desired a new home on higher ground that could take advantage of the views provided by the site. The existing home remains as a greeting house for visitors who come to see the sled dogs.

With simple materials of wood and concrete, mayer sattler-smith designed the new house – a wood-clad box with concrete forms. Blackened trees still dominate the area, and the exterior cladding of the house mimics the deep charcoal-black hue through the use of wood siding charred by the 1996 fire. Along the south side of the house, a 24-foot (7.5 meters) outer stairway leads from the lower level to a roof terrace with a single fir tree. An outside reflecting pool does double-duty as a water tank for a sprinkler system.

Inside, the rooms orient toward the views, with north-facing windows that provide a view of the expansive setting. A fireplace that provides vertical bracing on the main floor flanks a floor-to-ceiling window that reveals the valley. From the rooftop deck, the vista is even more stunning and vast.

The architects did not design to a construction budget since Buser did most of the actual building himself, trading sponsorship of his dog team for supplies and finding recycled materials or deals on his own. Instead, the architects designed a home that incorporates functional features and site-specific materials.

East façade.

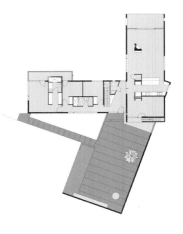

From above to below, from left to right:
South façade. Upper deck with views of Mount McKinley.
Floor plan. Front entrance.

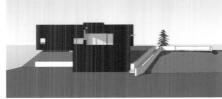

From above to below, from left to right:
South elevation. West elevation. South façade.

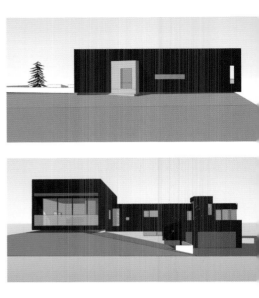

From above to below, from left to right:
View north and west from main living area. East eleva-
tion. North elevation. Main living area.

DAVIS RESIDENCE
ANCHORAGE, ALASKA / 2009

Anchorage was laid out by city planners in 1914, originally as a railroad construction port for the Alaska Railroad. In the 1940s and 1950s, Anchorage began looking more like a city. Between 1940 and 1951, Anchorage's population increased from 3,000 to 47,000. Several private residences were built in the city's "outskirts", although these areas today are considered part of the urban core.

Located in one of these early residential developments is this addition and renovation of a private residence, which pays homage to the existing 1950s ranch-style home; half of the original building was kept largely intact, including its interior, with a modern expansion added to the east side on top of the original foundation. The addition emphasizes contemporary design, public spaces and contact with nature. The site is in a neighborhood that used to be considered the edge of the city but now nestles at the edge of downtown. Most residents now live to the south of it.

Architects Bruce Williams and Michael Gerace of Black + White Studio Architects created spaces with large northern and southern windows, with views of the street along with a private backyard on the south side to take advantage of the southern exposure, the source of the warm sun in the subarctic climate. A large tree in the front yard increases privacy amidst the urban landscape, and stadium-sized steps at the back of the house lead gently from the kitchen to outdoor

places where the family can sit, eat lunch, and spend time with a surprising amount of privacy. Despite the contemporary nature of the addition, the home still respects the neighborhood vernacular.

In particular, the scale of the home is appropriate to the surrounding homes, and the chimney design reflects those of the neighboring houses. Natural light plays an important role in the home, with large windows carefully placed for transparency and southern exposure. A skylight in the kitchen opens views to a pine tree that extends from the backyard far above the house. The uniqueness of the Alaskan latitude means that the homeowners do not need to turn on many lights between April and August, when days are long.

At the same time, the quality of artificial light is very important during winter when interior lights are essential. Even the basement gets natural light, from exterior light openings that allow occupants to see out and light to enter. Even in winter, these windows remove the dampening sense of being underground and the low 7'3" (2.2 meters) basement ceilings.

Main living area.

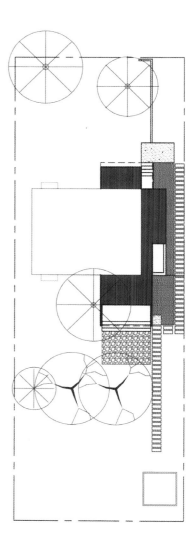

From above to below, from left to right:
View from main entrance. Site plan. South-facing façade.

From above to below, from left to right:
Floor plan, original structure. North elevation. View
towards south from main living area.

Koonce Pfeffer Bettis

VILLAGE SCHOOLS

AKIAK, AKIACHAK, TULUKSAK, AND KOTLIK, ALASKA / 2005

When designing three schools for the Yupiit School District and a fourth for the city of Kotlik in Alaska, Koonce Pfeffer Bettis had to consider the climate and logistical challenges of transporting supplies and materials to communities without road access. In these villages, where temperatures regularly reach -40° Fahrenheit (-40° Centigrade), the river serves as the main conduit of life.

Akiak is located at 60° 54' 36" N and has a total area of 3.1 square miles (8.0 square kilometers), of which, 2.0 square miles (5.1 square kilometers) of it is land and 1.1 square miles (2.8 square kilometers) of it (35.62%) is water. Located on the west bank of the Kuskokwim River, the village is 42 air miles (67 kilometers) northeast of Bethel, on the Yukon-Kuskokwim Delta. In 1880, the village of "Ackiagmute" had a population of 175. The name Akiak means "the other side", since this place was a crossing to the Yukon River basin during the winter for area Native Inupiaq. Nearby, 18 miles (28 kilometers) northeast of Bethel, is Akiachak, a village with a population was 585 and a total area of 6.8 square miles (17.5 square kilometers) of which, 6.8 square miles (17.5 square kilometers) of it is land and 0.15% is water. A federally-recognized tribe, the Akiachak Native Community, is located in the community. Akiachak is a Yup'ik village with a fishing and subsistence lifestyle. It has a strong traditional community, and was the first city in Alaska to dissolve its city government in favor of the Native village government. Tuluksak is located at 61 degrees latitude North,

with a population of 428 and a total area of 3.1 square miles of which, 3.0 square miles (7.9 square kilometers) of it is land and 0.1 square miles (0.2 square kilometers) of it (2.24%) is water. The three villages share a common climate. Precipitation averages 16 inches (0.40 meters), with snowfall of 50 inches (1.27 meters). Summer temperatures range from 42 to 62° Fahrenheit (5.5 to 16.6° Centigrade). Winter temperatures range from -2 to 19° Fahrenheit (-18.8 to 7.2° Centigrade). People get around by planes, snowmobiles, and boats, and a mail plane arrives every day with supplies and goods. The fuel trucks, water trucks, and cranes required on a construction project arrive on barges and return the next year, as the construction season is restricted to the short summer season. Anything not anticipated for construction is flown in at great cost and delay. Because low vegetation defines the landscape, large buildings are visible from one village to the next. Logistics may require thoughtful planning, and design considerations leave a lasting impression. Therefore, the design process includes many public meetings with community members and fullsite planning.

The three prototype schools in Akiak, Akiachuk, and Tuluksak take the basic form of a traditional native structure called the "qasgiq", or "men's house", a communal building where men lived and the Yup'ik people held ceremonies, dances, rituals, and seasonal activities.

Approach to main entrance.

An interpretation of the form, a wooden structure that forms a domelike shape, dominates the entrance of the schools in the Yup'ik district, each school separated from the other by 20 miles (32 kilometers), traversable by air or boat. They share the same basic plan with slightly different configurations, each housing 80 to 120 students and serving as a community hub and gathering place. The planning process for these projects included meetings with villagers, district officials, and elders.

The schools sit on steel piles with 48- to 60-inch (1.2- to 1.5-meter) water tables underneath them, which causes snow to blow under the buildings rather than forming drifts. Water tanks holding 10,000 to 15,000 gallons (37,853 to 56,779 liters) of water supply the sprinkler systems, and metal siding minimizes exterior maintenance. These are common construction methods in the North. Though isolated, these schools provide sophisticated educational experiences via Wi-Fi connectivity and trail systems for outdoor activities. The larger communal areas are separated from classroom wings, which also allows the village residents to use the schools for community activities all year long. The abundance of natural light that enters the spaces and the use of bold colors and natural wood materials throughout the interior create a warm, welcoming atmosphere during every season. Architectural elements, such as the arcs coming off the ends of the building, serve as snow fences to control drifting near entrances and windows. Materials used on the exterior, such as corrugated metal siding, were selected for their durability and low maintenance requirements.

For Kotlik School, extreme temperatures and snowdrift issues led to a simple exterior building form with simple rooflines and carefully chosen penetrations for energy efficiency. Kotlik is located at 63 degrees North latitude on the east bank of the Kotlik Sloughin the Yukon-Kuskokwim Delta. The city has a total area of 4.7 square miles (12 square kilometers), of which 3.8 square miles (9.9 square kilometers) of it

From above to below, from left to right:
Arctic fox outside Akiak School. Detail, façade, Akiak School. Façade, Akiakchak School. Connecting corridor, Akiak School.

is land and 0.8 square miles (2.1 square kilometers) of it (17.85%) is water. The climate of Kotlik is subarctic. Temperatures range between -50° and 87° Fahrenheit (-45° and 30° Centigrade). There is an average of 60 inches (1.5 meters) of snowfall and 16 inches (0.4 meters) of precipitation annually.

Inspiration for the Kotlik School design came again from the traditional Yup'ik "qasgiq", which was once the focus point of Native community life as the building functioned as a political and social center, guesthouse, sweat bath, and game and festival center. The two defined building volumes are connected with a bridge, one being the more "public" building with the entrance to school, multi-purpose room, gymnasium, kitchen, and library, and the other an educational wing with all the classrooms. The connecting bridge opens up with large windows highlighting the landscape and the winter sun. The building "pods" can operate independently, which allows for community use after school hours. The hallways wind like a river through the building, inspired by the local landscape, and also contrasts the strong lines of the exterior. The bilingual/bicultural classroom is visible throughout the school, providing a focal point inside and outside the building. The special classroom is entered through a long hallway, which opens into a large, open space. Outside the classroom is a wooden drying rack, a form reference to a common Native structure, offering connections to the traditional lifestyle.

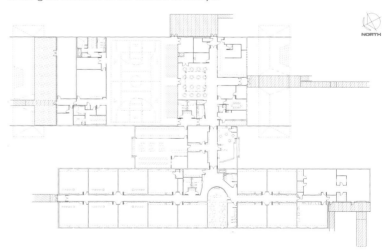

From above to below, from left to right:
Entrance Kotlik School. Exterior view by night from Kotlik School. Façade Kotlik School. Floor plan, Akiachak School. Exterior view Kotlik School.

66

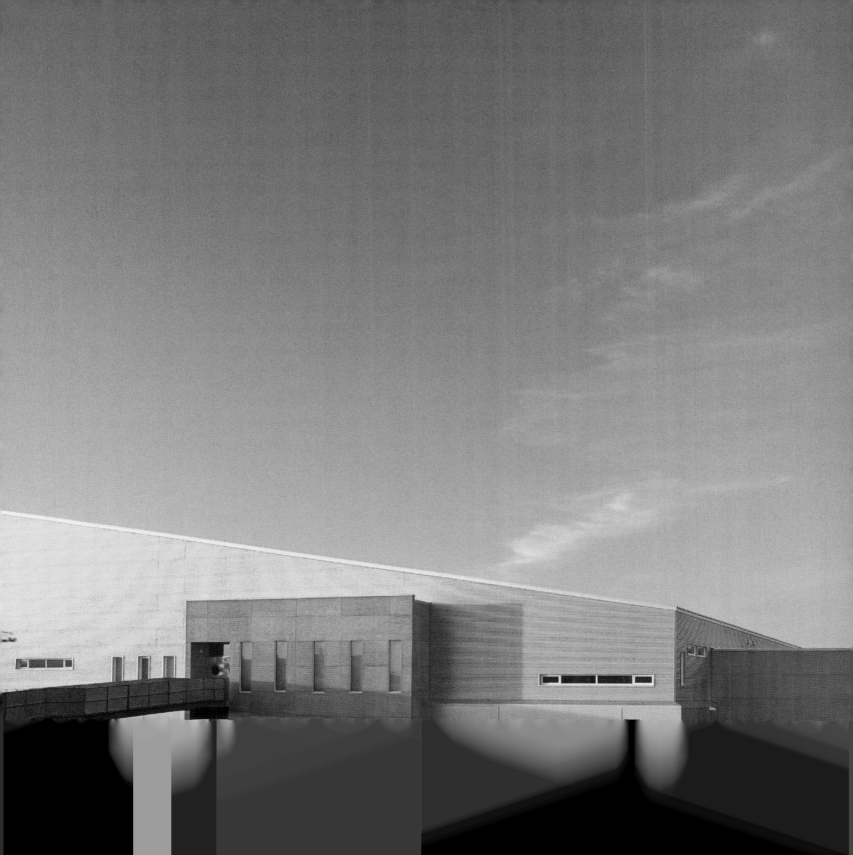

PHELPS/BURKE RESIDENCE

ANCHORAGE, ALASKA / 2004

The Phelps/Burke residence in south Anchorage is designed to maximize the view of Fire Island to the west and the mudflats and Cook Inlet to the south. Cook Inlet stretches 180 miles (290 kilometers) from the Gulf of Alaska to Anchorage in Southcentral Alaska. Cook Inlet branches into the Knik Arm and Turnagain Arm at its northern end, almost surrounding Anchorage.

The watershed covers about 100,000 square kilometers of southern Alaska, east of the Aleutian Range and south of the Alaska Range, including the drainage areas of Mount McKinley. Within the watershed there are several national parks and the active volcano Mount Redoubt, along with three other historically active volcanoes. Cook Inlet provides navigable access to the port of Anchorage at the northern end, and to the smaller Homer port further south.

The house's vantage point provides an ideal place to watch a dynamic landscape endlessly altered by the extreme tides and climate of Cook Inlet. Ten-foot ceiling heights and floor-to ceiling windows emphasize these perspectives while enhancing light and transparency.

The house sits on a pie-shaped lot – less than ideal for a traditional house – with a narrow footprint influenced by the clients' and architects' desire to spare two mature trees during construction. Though limited by these site constraints, the house's east-west orientation takes advantage of the southern exposure. Because the occupants spend a lot time out of state, they also wanted to be able to easily close up the house for long periods of time. The design embraces box forms and makes use of composite-material siding traditionally used for decking, largely in response to the clients' desire for a no-maintenance solution. Concrete floors offer a contemporary feel and continue the low-to-no maintenance approach. The public living space occupies the second floor of the house with a structural fireplace and eating nook off the kitchen. Wall-sized windows bring the outdoors in through light and a sense of open space. Windows on the top floor are sliding barndoor screens, allowing greater integration of the outdoors. The lower floor combines work space, bedrooms, and a guest room with movable partitions that allow one room to flow into the next or be closed off for privacy. These lower-floor bedrooms also offer seclusion from noise caused by high winds common to the region.

Outside spaces include a covered deck on the south and west sides of the upper level, as well as a north deck that offers a wind-sheltered space with a fireplace and barbeque. An elevated 15 feet x 15 feet (4.57 x 4.57 meters) studio, separate from the house, has 12 feet (3.65 meters) ceilings and provides a quiet space for creating artwork or listening to music.

View from northwest.

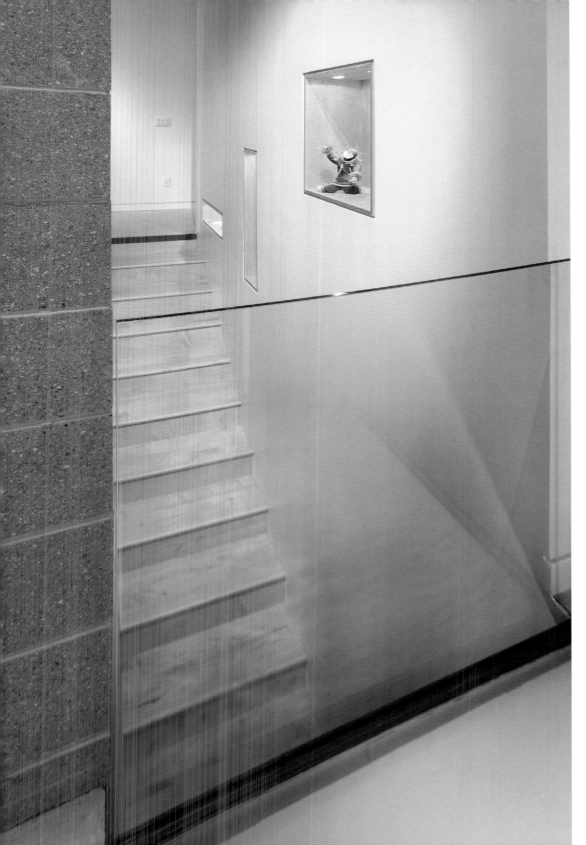

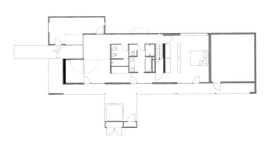

From above to below, from left to right:
Stair from main living area down to bedrooms and office.
Floor plan, level 1. Main living area with views of Cook
Inlet.

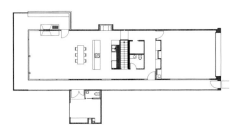

From above to below, from left to right:
Floor plan, level 2. Nord façade.

HOMER LIBRARY

HOMER, ALASKA / 2008

Homer is located at 59° 38' 35" N, on the shore of Kachemak Bay on the southwest side of the Kenai Peninsula. Its most distinguishing feature is the Homer Spit, a narrow 4.5 mile (7 kilometer) long gravel bar that extends into the bay, on which is located the Homer Harbor. Much of the coastline as well as the Homer Spit sank dramatically during the Good Friday Earthquake in March 1964. After the earthquake, very little vegetation was able to survive on the Homer Spit. One of Homer's nicknames is "the cosmic hamlet by the sea"; another is "the end of the road". A popular local bumper sticker characterizes the town as "Homer – A quaint little drinking village with a fishing problem".

This small seaside community with approximately 5,000 residents, is home to the newly constructed Homer Public Library. The site for 17,200-square-foot (1.600 square-meter) facility posed several unique challenges. Extreme temperatures, high wind loads and seasonal sunlight issues were important considerations for the design, engineering and construction of the project. With a long, narrow finger of land jutting 4.5 miles (29 kilometers) into the bay, Homer's geography played a critical role in the design considerations. Constructing an efficient building with numerous glazed elements had been a major challenge in the area, but the project architects wanted to push beyond the status quo of the "brick boxes" found in much of the region. Their design featured numerous glazed elements, including a curtain-walled

community reading room and multiple windows throughout. Solar heat gain was a critical issue for the project, as the angle of the sun and duration of sunlight varies greatly throughout the four seasons in Alaska. The summertime sun is high and can blaze for up to 19 hours a day, while in spring and fall, the sun is low and intense. In midwinter, the area can get as few as five hours of daylight in a 24-hour period. Another change came from the extreme wind loads associated with the area. Precise engineering and flawless fabrication were required to ensure the structure could withstand the elements.

To ensure efficiency, the designers employed a thermally broken curtain wall, windows, doors and framing. High-performance products helped to create a light-filled community reading room and provide abundant natural light throughout, without sacrificing thermal efficacy. Two rows of sun shades were incorporated into the curtain wall system, defending against solar heat gain and protecting the interior of the facility from the sun's harsh effects. The library was awarded LEED Silver certification by the U.S. Green Building Council and is only the third LEED building in Alaska and the second to achieve the silver rating. It is unique in being the first LEED building that arose from a community desire to address environmental sustainability.

West façade.

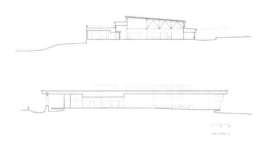

From above to below, from left to right:
Interior study areas. Floor plan. Building sections. South-west façade.

From above to below, from left to right:
Site plan. View from east.

MAASSEN/GOUWENS RESIDENCE

ANCHORAGE, ALASKA / 2009

At the base of the Chugach Mountains are the residential neighborhoods known as the "Hillside", where snow remains a bit longer than in the Anchorage "bowl", but residents have easy access to the Chugach State Park and numerous trails to the wildnerness, moose and bears in the backyard, and spectacular views of the city, Mount McKinley and the Alaska Range, volcanoes and the Cook Inlet.

The Maassen and Gouwens residence, designed by Anchorage-based Black + White Studio Architects, puts its occupants into a visceral relationship with the Chugach Mountains and an outdoor lifestyle. The building sits on a four-acre plot of land in between a mountain range and a valley – what the architects saw as a place of transition – with a creek running through the back side of the property. In this way, the house exists in transition as well – both in and out of the hill at the same time.

A detached garage – which many consider unusual or undesirable in the subarctic climate – serves as the entrance to the property. Though Anchorage residents depend on the automobile because of the vastness of the city limits and a lack of public transportations, the architects wanted to demonstrate that once you separate automobile from the place you live, it opens up the possibilities for architecture. A pathway leads away from the garage and past a small office, guest room, and then the main house, creating a mix of structures with out-door transition areas. Underneath the garage a recreation room provides a separate but connected space for teenagers. Lights lead from this garage/recreation area to the courtyard of the main house along a path that descends along the natural fall line of the hill. Expansive views dominate the 3,300-square-foot (306-square-meter) home and exposed timbers and ash wood floors in the living areas give it a spacious, woodsy look. Overall, the house is bright and light, particularly in the kitchen where natural light comes in from all directions.

Horses are kept on the property and can be seen from the bedrooms while two decks offer different experiences – one exposed to the elements for brilliant nights and warm summer days and the other as a covered shelter from the rain and snow. A rooftop garden offers a lookout from which to view an expanse of alders, the city of Anchorage in the distance and Cook Inlet beyond. Moose, bear, and small animals wander along the creek line.

View from southwest.

From above to below, from left to right:
Corridor leading to main living area. Site plan. Main living/dining area.

From above to below, from left to right:
Floor plan, level 1. Floor plan, level 2. Kitchen and main
living area.

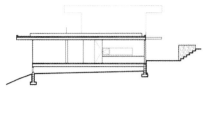
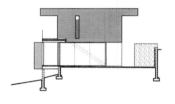

From above to below, from left to right:
Master bathroom. Elevations. Main living area.

RAVENWOOD VETERINARY CLINIC

EAGLE RIVER, ALASKA / 2009

Eagle River is a community within the Municipality of Anchorage, situated on the Eagle River, for which it is named, along the Chugach Mountains. If Eagle River were not part of the Municipality of Anchorage, it would be classified as one of the five largest cities in Alaska. Average temperatures in January range from 6 to 20° Fahrenheit (-14 to -6° Centigrade); in summer, temperatures range from 50 to 70° Fahrenheit (10 to 21° Centigrade). Annual precipitation is 15.9 inches (0.4 meters), with 69 inches (1.7 meters) of snowfall. The bulk of the snowfall is usually from mid-October through December, with fewer snowstorms from January through April. On average, the area experiences two to three "chinooks" – a warm, dry wind that melts much of the snow and creates a minor thaw – during the winter months. Springtime is generally referred to as "break up" in the area and further north, referring to the breaking up of the ice on rivers and lakes.

In this setting is the new Ravenwood veterinary clinic, a high-end building in the more urban area of Eagle River, although the backdrop is dominated by mountains that quickly rise up from the town. The building offers a play between inside and outside. Public functions such as the reception and waiting areas and the groomer's office open up to an entry courtyard. The spaces are open and inviting. The first floor houses all of the active animal care functions, including five exam rooms, a treatment area, a surgery center, x-ray lab, pharmacy and kennels. The second-floor houses more private functions such as doctors' offices and a staff lounge area, which opens up to an exterior deck.

To be compatible with its urban surroundings, the building's form is defined through rectangular shapes. The exterior is clad in dark metal skin, which also wraps around the courtyard areas, including an outdoor area with kennels. The materiality is highlighted with a play of light through a perforation of the metal skin the courtyard areas. The effect of light permeating the skin also allows the building to change appearance from day to night. To meet the client's need for low-maintenance materials in high-use areas, mayer-sattler smith employed interior finishes such as exposed concrete flooring and wood walls and ceilings. Seamless rubber flooring is used in treatment and surgery rooms and hospital fixtures are stainless steel. To allow for natural light, floor-to-ceiling windows open up the interior to the courtyards.

Southwest façade at dusk.

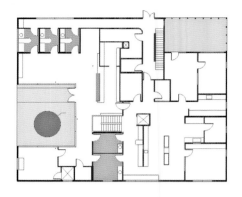

From above to below, from left to right:
Main entrance area. Floor plan, level 1. Main entry.

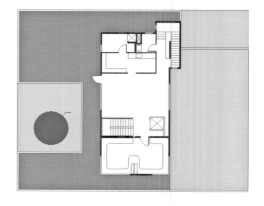

From above to below, from left to right:
Exterior walkway. Floor plan, level 2. Main entrance.

CREDITS

Foreword
Picture Credit / MAPS.com/CORBIS, MG003314

Introduction
Picture Credits / Chris Arend Photography (15 a., 16 a.), Bettmann/CORBIS, U1309563INP (7 a.), Bettmann/CORBIS, BE042141 (10 a.), Bettmann/CORBIS, U1104179INP (12 b.), Bettmann/CORBIS, BE025824 (13 a.), Bettmann/CORBIS, U1064503 (13 m. a.), Don DeVoe (14 m.), Hal Gage (15 m., 16 m., 16 b., 17 a., 17 b., 18, 19 a., 19 m. b.), Ann Johansson/Corbis, 42-16055848 (10 m. a.), Karen Larsen (17 m.), Michael Maslan Historic Photographs/CORBIS, IH032846 (12 m. b.), Courtesy of Morphosis (15 b.), Kevin G. Smith (7 m., 7 b., 8, 9, 10 m. b., 10 b., 11, 12 a., 12 m. a., 13 m. b., 13 b., 14 a., 14 b., 19 m. a., 19 b., 20)

Concieving an Alaskan Tradition
Picture Credits / Ann Johansson/Corbis, 42-16359884 (23 m.), Steven Kazlowski/Science Faction/Corbis, 42-21866706 (22 b.), Steven Kazlowski/Science Faction/Corbis, 42-21868785 (23 a.), Kevin G. Smith (21, 22 a., 22 m., 23 b.)

Nearpoint Residence
Owner/Client / Richard Navitsky & Tanya Leinicke
Architect / Workshop for Architecture and Design
Project Team / Steven Bull, Dan Rusler,
Marty McElveen
Consultants / Harriott Engineers
Photography / Kevin G. Smith
Plans / Courtesy of Workshop for Architecture and Design

BP Energy Center
Client / BP Exploration Alaska, Inc.
Architect and Interior Design / Koonce Pfeffer Bettis
General Contractor / Boslough Construction
Mechanical Engineering / Hay, Zietlow and Associates
Electrical Engineering / EIC
Civil Engineering / DOWL Engineers
Structural Engineering / PDC
Exhibit Consultants / Ear Studio
Photography / Kevin G. Smith (36 a., 36 b.), Don Mohr (35, 36 m., 37, 38, 39)

Anchorage Museum at Rasmuson Center, New Wing
Client / Anchorage Museum
Design Architect / David Chipperfield Architects
Architect of Record / Kumin Associates Incorporated
Landscape Architect / Charles Anderson Landscape Architecture
Consulting Landscape Architect / Earthscape
Structural Engineering / BBFM Engineers Inc.
Associate Structural Engineering /
Magnusson Klemencic Associates, Inc.
MEP & IT Engineer of Record / Affiliated Engineers NW, Inc.
MEP Engineer of Record / RSA Engineering, Inc.
Civil Engineering / Tryck Nyman Hayes, Inc.
Geotechnical Engineering / DOWL HKM Engineers